The Kardashian Look

Destiny S. Harris

. . .

1st Free Gift!

Giving Rocks.

I give away free books daily. Get your free books today. Here's how

Step 1: Visit amazon.com/author/destinyharris

Step 2: Filter books by "Price: Low to High"

Step 3: Download available free books

. . .

Table of Contents

. . .

. . .

What Is The Kardashian Look?

Has anyone noticed that many women are starting (or already do) to look the same?

I call it the **Kardashian** look.

Three specific traits that come with the Kardashian look are:

1. The oversized ss, with stick legs.

2. The juiced-up lips that don't look natural.

3. A perfectly contoured, air-brushed face is usually covered in "natural-esque" makeup.

4. Larger chests that are usually not natural and appear perfectly symmetrical.

5. Thick and air-brush-like eyebrows (tattooing eyebrows is becoming more popular to maintain this look).

. . .

Is The Kardashian Look Wrong?

Not necessarily.

Everyone has and deserves the right to look how they want.

But I find it intriguing that many women emulate this look and deviate from their natural looks.

Though most people still have not attained plastic surgery, more and more people are obtaining plastic surgical procedures due to increased accessibility.

Lips jobs, boob jobs, tummy tucks, butt jobs, and lift jobs are all becoming cheaper.

. . .

Why Go For The Kardashian Look?

There are a couple of reasons to go for the Kardashian look:

1. Since the Kardashians embody: beauty, wealth, power, and popularity, it is no wonder that the average person would also want to look like them.

2. Many men *and* women find the Kardashian look attractive.

Most people want to appear attractive to others. If the Kardashian look equates to attraction, more people will aim to make their look similar.

3. With plastic surgery being more accessible, people can enhance their bodies on demand.

The other side of this: Many people cover their surgical costs with debt or loans. The cost of beauty goes deep.

. . .

The Kardashian Norm

Natural beauty might become an "endangered species."

Depending on where you live, you might notice that many women around you are starting to look like the same person.

There are two primary looks:

1. Natural
2. Unnatural

I'm observing the unnatural look more and more in my daily experience.

With increasing access to plastic surgery, the perpetuation of unattainable beauty standards, and the growing desire to emulate success in all forms, we will probably continue to see a shift in women looking the same.

. . .

Who Is Perpetuating The Kardashian Look?

We are.

Many people blame men for perpetuating beauty standards, but the truth is we are the culprits because we are the ones changing our physical bodies.

To be continued.

. . .

About Destiny S. Harris

Destiny S. Harris' goal is to positively inspire, cultivate, elevate, and educate the minds of individuals across the globe through her writing.

Creating (whether books, courses, articles, poetry, or music) has always been Destiny's thing, not to mention health & fitness and all things entrepreneurial. Destiny published her first book, "Beauty Secrets for Girls," at age 11 and her second book, "Don't Wait Until It's Too Late," at age 12.

Destiny obtained three degrees from the University of Georgia in Psychology, Political Science, & Cultural Studies. She also started her own music teaching business at the age of 14, which she led for over ten years. In addition, she has been teaching academic, career, and personal development topics to thousands of students and readers since 2004.

Outside of writing, Destiny loves and enjoys a few other things: reading, bodybuilding, traveling, dogs, food, classic movies, anime, mountain and ocean views, plants, and nature.

Check out her work, leave a review, share your thoughts with your friends and family, and be a part of a movement: helping people learn and grow through means of self-education (books).

<u>Complete the Steps To Get Free eBooks:</u>

Step 1: Go to amazon.com/author/destinyharris

Step 2: Filter books by "Price: Low to High"

Step 3: Download available free books

Connect W/ Destiny S. Harris

Please reach out and stay in touch. Destiny S. Harris enjoys chatting with readers.

Start a conversation today @ destinyh.com

Free Gifts!

Access free courses & books at the link below:

destinyh.com